A LOOK AT CONTINENTS
EXPLORE AFRICA

by Veronica B. Wilkins

Ideas for Parents and Teachers

Pogo Books let children practice reading informational text while introducing them to nonfiction features such as headings, labels, sidebars, maps, and diagrams, as well as a table of contents, glossary, and index.

Carefully leveled text with a strong photo match offers early fluent readers the support they need to succeed.

Before Reading

- "Walk" through the book and point out the various nonfiction features. Ask the student what purpose each feature serves.
- Look at the glossary together. Read and discuss the words.

Read the Book

- Have the child read the book independently.
- Invite him or her to list questions that arise from reading.

After Reading

- Discuss the child's questions. Talk about how he or she might find answers to those questions.
- Prompt the child to think more. Ask: Most of Africa has two seasons. They are the rainy season and the dry season. What are the seasons like where you live?

Pogo Books are published by Jump!
5357 Penn Avenue South
Minneapolis, MN 55419
www.jumplibrary.com

Library of Congress Cataloging-in-Publication Data

Names: Wilkins, Veronica B., 1994- author.
Title: Explore Africa / Veronica B. Wilkins.
Description: Minneapolis, MN: Jump!, [2020]
Series: A look at continents | Pogo Books
Audience: Ages 7-10 | Audience: Grades 2-3
Identifiers: LCCN 2019029473 (print)
LCCN 2019029474 (ebook)
ISBN 9781645272823 (hardcover)
ISBN 9781645272830 (paperback)
ISBN 9781645272847 (ebook)
Subjects: LCSH: Africa–Juvenile literature.
Classification: LCC DT22 .W49 2020 (print)
LCC DT22 (ebook) | DDC 960–dc23
LC record available at https://lccn.loc.gov/2019029473
LC ebook record available at https://lccn.loc.gov/2019029474

Editor: Susanne Bushman
Designer: Michelle Sonnek

Photo Credits: kyslynskahal/Shutterstock, cover; i_am_zews/Shutterstock, 1; Carl Dupont/Shutterstock, 3; Jeffrey B. Banke/Shutterstock, 4; guenterhuni/iStock, 5; Maciej Es/Shutterstock, 6-7 (foreground); Jaroslav74/Shutterstock, 6-7 (background); Nick Fox/Shutterstock, 8-9; Andrzej Kubik/Shutterstock, 10-11, 14-15; Francois Gagnon/Shutterstock, 12; GUDKOV ANDREY/Shutterstock, 13; Marion Couturier/Shutterstock, 16-17; Tykhanskyi Viacheslav/Shutterstock, 18; bolarzeal/Shutterstock, 19; iSelena/Shutterstock, 20-21; Kwadrat/Shutterstock, 23.

Printed in the United States of America at Corporate Graphics in North Mankato, Minnesota.

TABLE OF CONTENTS

CHAPTER 1

A LARGE PLATEAU

Let's explore the **continent** of Africa! Lions, hyenas, giraffes, and many other animals roam the Serengeti **Plain**.

Nile
River

The Nile River is here. It is the longest river in the world! Is it 4,132 miles (6,650 kilometers) long. It flows north. Only a few rivers in the world do this.

Africa is a large continent. Of the seven, only Asia is larger. The **equator** runs through Africa. This imaginary line divides Earth. Africa is in both the Northern and Southern **Hemispheres**.

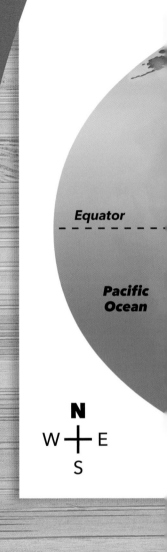

Equator

Pacific
Ocean

N
W — E
S

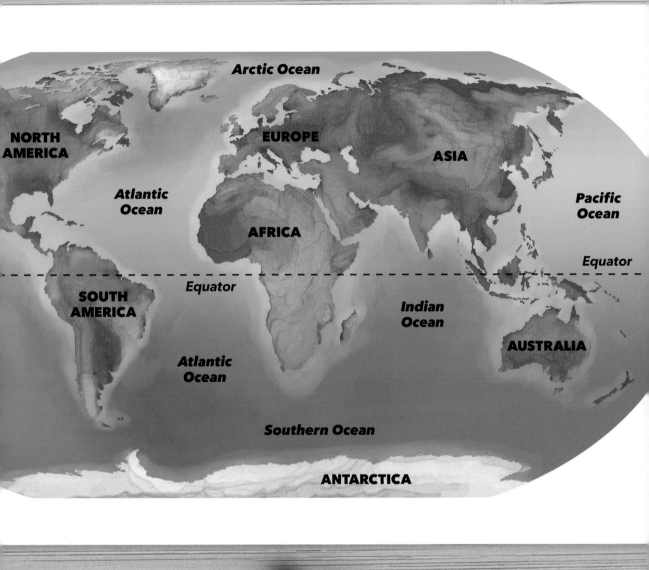

Arctic Ocean

EUROPE

ASIA

NORTH
AMERICA

Atlantic
Ocean

Pacific
Ocean

AFRICA

Equator

Equator

SOUTH
AMERICA

Indian
Ocean

AUSTRALIA

Atlantic
Ocean

Southern Ocean

ANTARCTICA

Great Rift Valley

The continent has many large **plateaus**. The Atlas Mountains are in the northwest. The Great Rift Valley is in the east. Rift valleys are long, low areas of land. They form when **tectonic plates** move apart.

There are many rivers and lakes here, too. Lake Victoria is the largest lake in Africa. The Nile River, Niger River, and Congo River are important rivers.

DID YOU KNOW?

The Great Rift Valley could be full of water one day! Why? Tectonic plates keep moving apart. The rift could spread to the ocean.

Mount Kilimanjaro is the highest point in Africa. It is 19,340 feet (5,895 meters) high. It is the tallest mountain in the world that is not in a mountain range. People come from around the world to hike to the top.

WHAT DO YOU THINK?

Mount Kilimanjaro has ice on top. But it is melting. Why do you think this is? Can you think of other places where the landscape has changed?

Mount
Kilimanjaro

CHAPTER 2

A TROPICAL CONTINENT

Africa's two seasons are the dry and rainy seasons. About half the continent is **savanna**. Wildebeests live here. They **migrate** to places with green grasses to eat.

Africa's rain forests have more than 10,000 species of **tropical** plants. Gorillas live in the rain forests.

Ostriches live in the savanna. They are the biggest birds in the world. They can be about 9 feet (2.7 m) tall! They don't fly. Why? Their wings are too small. They run instead.

The **climate** here is mostly tropical. Why? Weather around the equator does not change much. The Sahara Desert is in northern Africa. The Kalahari Desert is in the south.

Sahara Desert

TAKE A LOOK!

What different climate **regions** are in Africa? Take a look!

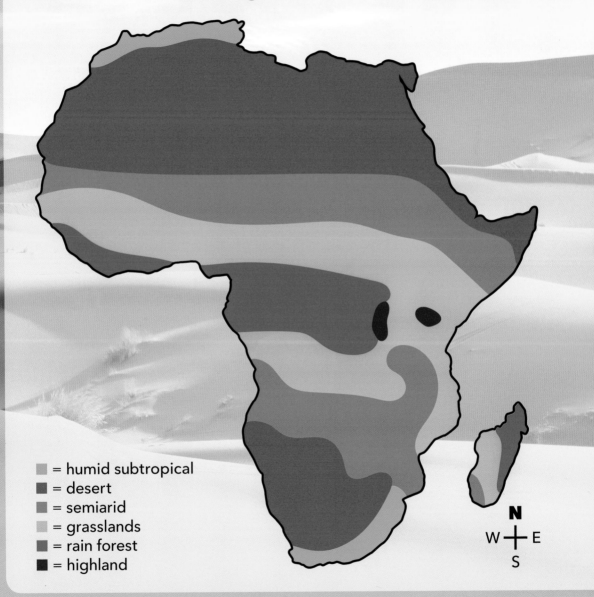

= humid subtropical
= desert
= semiarid
= grasslands
= rain forest
= highland

N
W—E
S

CHAPTER 3
LIFE IN AFRICA

People in Africa choose where to live based on climate. Few people live in deserts. Why? It is very hot and dry. Most live near lakes and rivers. These provide water for people, animals, and **crops**.

The country here with the most people is Nigeria. Around 200 million people live in Nigeria! Lagos is here. It is Africa's largest city.

Lagos, Nigeria

There are thousands of **ethnic** groups here. Between 900 and 1,500 languages are spoken! Most people speak more than one.

Africa is a continent full of **diverse** people! They live in many climates and landscapes. Would you like to explore Africa?

WHAT DO YOU THINK?

Europeans **colonized** much of Africa. When? They began in the 1800s. They made country borders. Do you think Africans would have drawn different borders?

QUICK FACTS & TOOLS

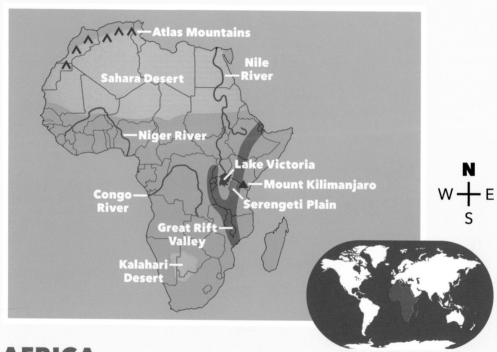

Atlas Mountains

Nile River

Sahara Desert

Niger River

Lake Victoria

Mount Kilimanjaro

Congo River

Serengeti Plain

Great Rift Valley

Kalahari Desert

N
W E
S

AFRICA

Size: 12 million square miles (31 million square km)

Size Rank: Asia, **Africa**, North America, South America, Antarctica, Europe, Australia

Population Estimate: 1.2 billion people (2019 estimate)

Exports: petroleum, minerals, cotton, sugar, coffee

Facts: Africa makes up about 20 percent of Earth's land.

The Sahara Desert is almost the size of the United States.

GLOSSARY

climate: The weather typical of a certain place over a long period of time.

colonized: Established a new settlement.

continent: One of the seven large landmasses of Earth.

crops: Plants grown for food.

diverse: Having many different types or kinds.

equator: An imaginary line around the middle of Earth that is an equal distance from the North and South Poles.

ethnic: Of or having to do with a group of people sharing the same national origins, language, or culture.

hemispheres: Halves of a round object, especially of Earth.

migrate: To move from one region or habitat to another.

plain: A large, flat area of land.

plateaus: Areas of level ground that are higher than the surrounding area.

regions: General areas or specific districts or territories.

savanna: A flat, grassy plain with few or no trees.

tectonic plates: Massive, irregularly shaped slabs of rock that are deep underground and move slowly, changing Earth's landscape.

tropical: Of or having to do with the hot, rainy areas of the tropics.

INDEX

TO LEARN MORE

Finding more information is as easy as 1, 2, 3.

❶ Go to www.factsurfer.com

❷ Enter "exploreAfrica" into the search box.

❸ Choose your book to see a list of websites.

FACT SURFER